UNDER
WEAR

A very peculiar history

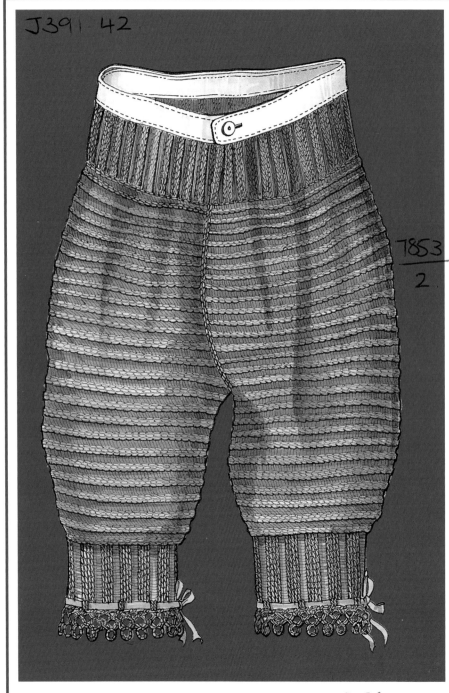

SERIES EDITOR	DAVID SALARIYA
BOOK EDITOR	PENNY CLARKE
ASSISTANT	APRIL MCCROSKIE
ARTISTS	DAVID ANTRAM
	RAY BURROWS
	VIRGINIA GRAY
	JOHN JAMES
	JOE MCEWAN
	LEE PETERS
	RON TINER
	GERALD WOOD

DAVID SALARIYA was born in Dundee, Scotland, where he studied illustration and printmaking. He has illustrated a wide range of books and has created many new series of books for publishers in the UK and overseas. In 1989 he established the Salariya Book Company. He lives in Brighton with his wife, the illustrator Shirley Willis.

JENNIFER RUBY has written and illustrated 20 books on the history of costume, and regularly gives talks on costume in schools and runs art workshops for children and adults. She lives and works in Hertfordshire, where she also holds exhibitions of her watercolours.

First published in 1995
by Watts Books

Watts Books
96 Leonard Street
London EC2A 4RH

© The Salariya Book Co Ltd MCMXCV

ISBN 0 7496 1284 3

Printed in Belgium

A CIP catalogue record for this book is available from the British Library.

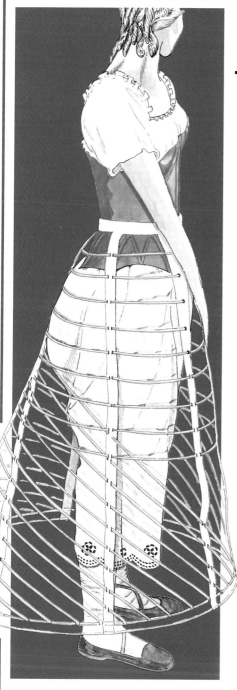

UNDER
WEAR

A very peculiar history

Written by
JENNIFER RUBY

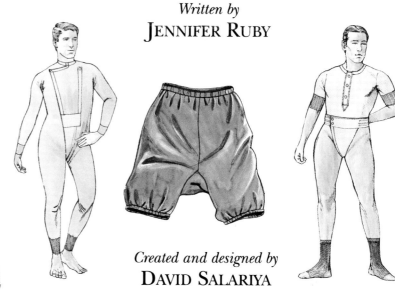

Created and designed by
DAVID SALARIYA

WATTS BOOKS

LONDON NEW YORK SYDNEY

Contents

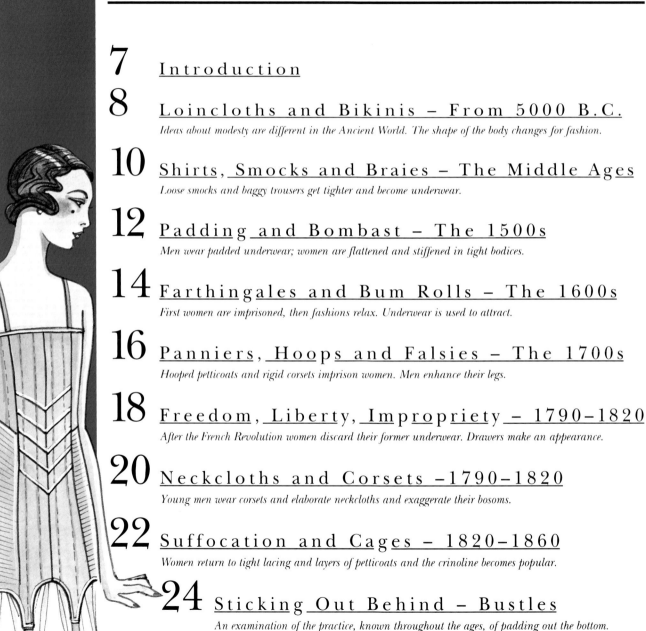

INTRODUCTION

THROUGHOUT THE AGES, underwear has had several different functions, the first of these being protection. It protects the body from cold and also provides some degree of modesty for the wearer. In centuries past it was also used to protect outerwear. Personal hygiene was not considered important and the beautiful fabrics used for clothing needed protection from the filthy skin of the wearer!

Secondly, underwear can change a person's shape, giving him or her the silhouette that is currently fashionable. This is done by paring down or adding on. Paring down can be agony and is accomplished through bandaging, boning and tight lacing. Adding on is achieved through ingenious padding, stuffing and other mysterious appliances. Indeed, some of the fantastically exaggerated shapes of costumes of the past could not have been achieved without some very unusual undergarments to support them.

Thirdly, underclothing has also been used as a method of class distinction. The frills and lace on the shirt of a 17th-century gentleman would clearly distinguish him from the manual worker who wore only a plain, practical garment.

Another interesting phenomenon is the way in which outergarments become undergarments and vice versa. For example, the tightly laced bodices on medieval gowns became the corsets of later years and, in modern times, clothes designers have frequently used underwear as outerwear.

Underwear is a fascinating subject, with a very peculiar history . . .

LOINCLOTHS AND BIKINIS – FROM 5000 B.C.

Ancient civilizations begin to control their figures.

Terracotta figure of a Babylonian girl wearing briefs, c.3000 B.C.

An Egyptian pharaoh c.3000 B.C. wearing only a pleated loincloth. Eventually, the tunic developed from the loincloth, which was extended up to the shoulder and down to the feet. His beard would be false, and stuck on for a festive occasion.

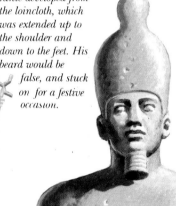

Cretan snake goddess, 2000 B.C., with a "wasp" waist.

Phoenician woman with ballooning skirts but again no covering for the chest.

WHEN WE THINK OF UNDERWEAR today, we tend to think of garments that provide some degree of modesty for the wearer and shape and control the figure. If we look back in time, it is clear that ancient civilizations took a very different view. Early records of clothing show evidence of loincloths and what we would call briefs. These garments would be outerwear rather than underwear and as the chest was left bare, we must assume that if there were any sense of modesty at this time it did not apply to the upper part of the body!

People soon learned to alter their natural shape, however, and figures from Crete and Mycenae indicate a fashion for tiny waists which must have been artificially achieved. There is literary evidence also that the ancient Greeks had some form of figure control. A zoné or girdle was a band of material worn around the waist in order to control it, and breast bands were worn to flatten and minimize the bust. Gradually, as more layers of clothing were worn, what had originally been outerwear became underwear and so our story begins . . .

Cretan priest-king, c.1500 B.C. Like the snake goddess, he has an extremely narrow waist, which could only have been achieved by wearing a very rigid girdle from childhood.

pleated loincloth

(Below) A Roman woman dressed for gymnastics in what we would call a bikini. The strophium, or breast band, was sometimes used like a pocket.

An Egyptian queen in a tight-fitting robe called a kalasaris. It was cut from pieces of cloth that were sewn together at the sides. An undergarment with shoulder straps is visible beneath.

(Left) This Egyptian woman is wearing a tunic with a shoulder strap. It would be of fine cotton. Her body would be anointed with oils.

kalasaris

tunic

(Above) A Greek woman binding her breasts. The wool or linen binding was called a fascia.

(Left) An Egyptian courtesan, 5th century B.C. Her garment seems more attractive than practical.

strophium

dancer

Egyptian dancer, acrobat and musician. These slave girls entertained guests at feasts. Their clothing was as much for ornament as modesty.

acrobat

musician

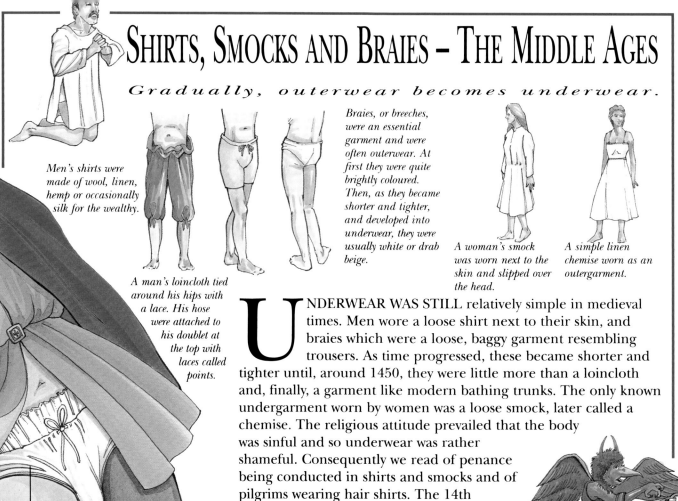

SHIRTS, SMOCKS AND BRAIES – THE MIDDLE AGES

Gradually, outerwear becomes underwear.

Men's shirts were made of wool, linen, hemp or occasionally silk for the wealthy.

A man's loincloth tied around his hips with a lace. His hose were attached to his doublet at the top with laces called points.

Braies, or breeches, were an essential garment and were often outerwear. At first they were quite brightly coloured. Then, as they became shorter and tighter, and developed into underwear, they were usually white or drab beige.

A woman's smock was worn next to the skin and slipped over the head.

A simple linen chemise worn as an outergarment.

loincloth

points

UNDERWEAR WAS STILL relatively simple in medieval times. Men wore a loose shirt next to their skin, and braies which were a loose, baggy garment resembling trousers. As time progressed, these became shorter and tighter until, around 1450, they were little more than a loincloth and, finally, a garment like modern bathing trunks. The only known undergarment worn by women was a loose smock, later called a chemise. The religious attitude prevailed that the body was sinful and so underwear was rather shameful. Consequently we read of penance being conducted in shirts and smocks and of pilgrims wearing hair shirts. The 14th century saw the beginning of fashion as we know it today. Garments became more sophisticated and changed shape more often. It is uncertain whether women wore corsets, but some earlier gowns appear so tight that they suggest at least some kind of bandaging beneath. Later in the period laced bodices ensured figure-hugging clothes for women.

The Winchester Psalter of 1150 depicts the devil as a woman. Her tight-fitting laced bodice suggests that women were already distorting their figures for fashion.

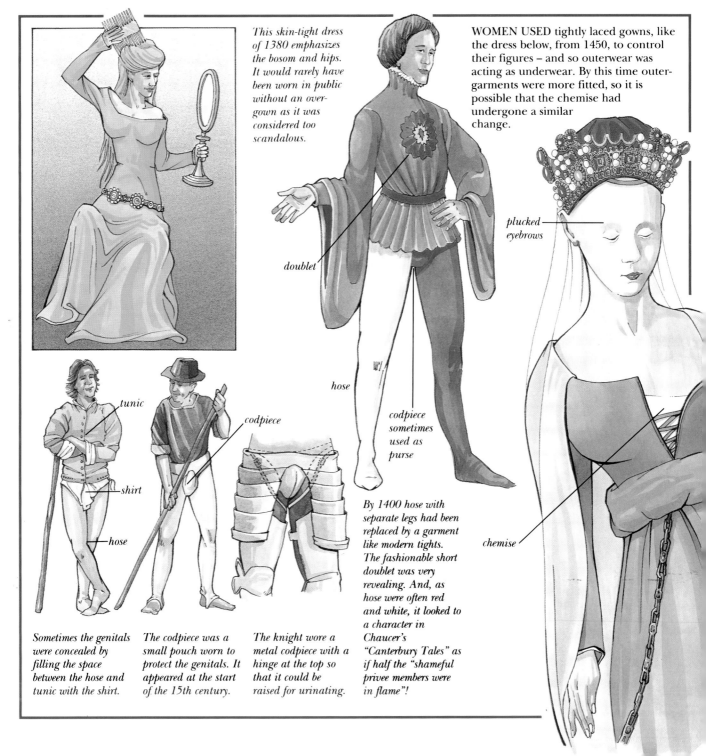

This skin-tight dress of 1380 emphasizes the bosom and hips. It would rarely have been worn in public without an over-gown as it was considered too scandalous.

WOMEN USED tightly laced gowns, like the dress below, from 1450, to control their figures – and so outerwear was acting as underwear. By this time outer-garments were more fitted, so it is possible that the chemise had undergone a similar change.

doublet

hose

codpiece sometimes used as purse

tunic

shirt

hose

codpiece

plucked eyebrows

chemise

Sometimes the genitals were concealed by filling the space between the hose and tunic with the shirt.

The codpiece was a small pouch worn to protect the genitals. It appeared at the start of the 15th century.

The knight wore a metal codpiece with a hinge at the top so that it could be raised for urinating.

By 1400 hose with separate legs had been replaced by a garment like modern tights. The fashionable short doublet was very revealing. And, as hose were often red and white, it looked to a character in Chaucer's "Canterbury Tales" as if half the "shameful privee members were in flame"!

PADDING AND BOMBAST – THE 1500s

New, artificial shapes no longer follow the body's line.

THE 16TH CENTURY is often considered to be the beginning of the modern period. The world was opening up and it was a time of expansion, extravagance and ostentatious display. Clothes reflected status and material well-being. During the first half of the century men's fashions stressed power and virility. Square, padded shoulders gave an aggressive, masculine look and the codpiece, also padded, became large and decorative. Women's clothes were quite modest by comparison, with soft, flowing lines. Underneath, they were now wearing petticoats. The second half of the century saw a startling turnabout. Women's fashions changed from lines that followed the natural body shape to created, artificial forms. The chest and stomach were flattened, with stiffened bodices or with corsets, and the Spanish farthingale held out skirts in bell-like shapes. At the same time, men began to emphasize their waists and pad out their hips.

The collar on men's shirts began to move upwards. It was to become more elaborate and develop into the fashionable ruff of later in the century.

chemise

codpiece

garters

padded hose

The bulky, aggressive look epitomized by Henry VIII of England was adopted by fashionable men in the 16th century.

Men's hose were divided into two parts, upper and lower. The upper part gradually became more bulbous and

was filled with padding known as bombast. Stockings, which were worn over hose, were held up with garters.

The chemise has been pulled through the slashes on the sleeves and is also visible at the neck. Petticoats would be worn beneath and tied to the body with laces.

A STIFF, STARCHED RUFF, a padded belly (called a peasecod belly), hose stuffed with bombast to emphasize the hips, and a decorated codpiece comprise the more effeminate look of later in the century (below). This reversal from a masculine to a more feminine look can be attributed partly to the move from male to female power in the reign of Elizabeth I, who was such a dominant figure in Europe.

(Above) The Spanish farthingale was similar to the dress of the Cretan snake goddess on page 8. The hoops were made of cane, whalebone or wire.

A bodice stiffened with whalebone or metal was often worn under the dress and was called a "body".

ruff

peasecod belly

codpiece

Iron corsets from the early 16th century, probably designed for difficult or deformed figures.

(Below) The development of the peasecod belly. It was achieved with a stuffing of flax or hemp.

The lower classes did not follow these rigid fashions, as they were too expensive and impractical. However, women still laced up their figures even for working. The man is wearing short stockings and garters.

FARTHINGALES AND BUM ROLLS – THE 1600s

Underclothes are used to denote social class and to attract.

Though imprisoned in a lace ruff, this lady has her chest exposed.

The French farthingale, introduced towards the end of the 16th century, made the skirt stand out like a cartwheel from the waist.

stiffened bodice

petticoat hoops

DURING THE 17TH CENTURY underwear developed a new significance in that it ceased to be merely functional. Men's garments were used to denote social status and women's to look attractive. A man's shirt was consciously displayed as the mark of a fine gentleman and, as women's fashions changed from rigid to more flowing lines, there was a greater chance of a provocative glimpse of petticoat, which became a recognized symbol of feminine charm. After the disappearance of the farthingale, women wore three petticoats to support their skirts.

Corsets were used to mould the bust and the first publicity slogan for underwear appeared in the window of a corset maker: "It controls the large, supports the small and uplifts the drooping"! As men and women were usually dirty and often verminous, undergarments were heavily perfumed to distract from disagreeable odours and make the wearer more attractive.

ruff

A dress worn over a farthingale (left).

(Right) Some women preferred the less cumbersome "bum roll" to the farthingale. This was a roll of padding worn beneath the skirt at the hips and tied at the front with laces.

bum roll

Early 17th-century bodice boned with wood or whalebone and covered with linen or damask.

The bodice of a dress might be so rigid that no corset was needed; so outerwear was serving as underwear.

shirt

drawers

SHIRT AND DRAWERS, 1686. Lace ruffles would be attached to the wristbands of the shirt. Sometimes they covered the hands, a sign of superior rank.

feather

This beribboned mid-century gentleman is fashionably un-buttoned at various strategic places, displaying his fine underwear.

ribbon

lace

shirt

unbuttoned breeches

lace

Nell Gwynne (left), mistress of Charles II of England. Exposing the forearms was considered shocking.

(Below) Neckwear continued to be im-portant. As ruffs dis-appeared, cravats became fashionable.

Steinkirk cravat

(Below) Indecent exposure! Both male and female wear stockings, garters and lace. The lady would not be wearing any drawers, as these were considered immodest.

stockings

garters

Panniers, Hoops and Falsies – The 1700s

Rigid, tight fashions are achieved with hoops, stays and padding.

White stockings became fashionable.

A hoop petticoat gave the overskirt a bell shape.

THE 18TH CENTURY is usually considered an age of elegance. Everything was precise, controlled and orderly and this was reflected in the rigidity of the fashions. For most of this period women's dress was dominated by the hoop petticoat, which changed shape several times. The difference between wearing this and the earlier farthingale was that dress materials were now much lighter. The hoop therefore moved very easily, exposing the legs which had become the new centre of attraction. After the hoop petticoat's disappearance, lift was given to the back of the dress by means of false "rumps" or "bums". Corsets and stays were tightly laced and compressed the stomach, pushed the bosom forward and held the shoulders back.

Men's underwear began to fade into insignificance and was no longer worn with the intent of being attractive. This was partly due to tighter-fitting clothes which left little opportunity to display undergarments. However, the shirt front and cuffs were still an indication of class. Improved standards of cleanliness meant that hot water and soap were more generally used for washing underwear, though it was still difficult to clean stays. Contemporary sources reported that working-class women often wore leather stays until they rotted, without ever washing them.

tie

hoop

petticoat

Panniers (above) extended the hips to the side but made the front and back appear flat.

As the fashion for side hoops became more exaggerated, dresses could be 120-180 centimetres wide, so women took up a great deal of space when they moved.

panier

busk

WEARERS NEEDED MUCH dexterity to pass through doorways and narrow streets and climb into carriages.

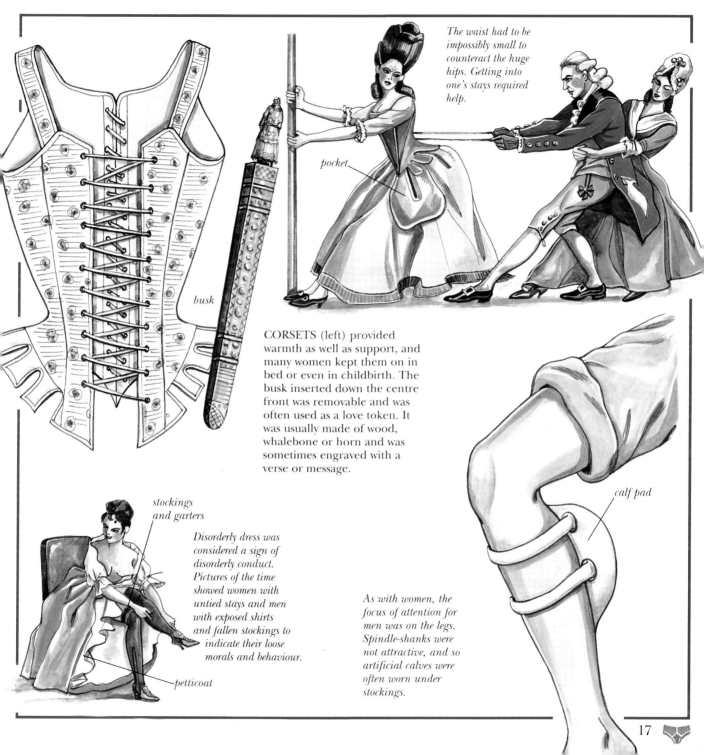

The waist had to be impossibly small to counteract the huge hips. Getting into one's stays required help.

busk

pocket

CORSETS (left) provided warmth as well as support, and many women kept them on in bed or even in childbirth. The busk inserted down the centre front was removable and was often used as a love token. It was usually made of wood, whalebone or horn and was sometimes engraved with a verse or message.

calf pad

stockings
and garters

Disorderly dress was considered a sign of disorderly conduct. Pictures of the time showed women with untied stays and men with exposed shirts and fallen stockings to indicate their loose morals and behaviour.

petticoat

As with women, the focus of attention for men was on the legs. Spindle-shanks were not attractive, and so artificial calves were often worn under stockings.

17

FREEDOM, LIBERTY, IMPROPRIETY – 1790–1820

Discarding their former underwear, women appear semi-naked beneath their clothes.

The high-waisted, classical style that followed the French Revolution. The dress would be made of muslin or cotton lawn.

WITH ITS CRY OF FREEDOM, liberty and equality, the French Revolution of 1789 seemed to bring about a revolution in fashion. As the old, rigid class system collapsed, so did the rigid fashions that had mirrored it. Hoops, petticoats and corsets were discarded and instead there was a vogue for slim, high-waisted muslin or cotton gowns that clung to the figure and were worn with the minimum of underclothing. This classical style, inspired by Greek statues, was considered a classless mode of dress, though it was hardly suitable for milking cows! Underwear was reduced to a single narrow petticoat and there were rumours that some devotees of the fashion dampened their dresses to make them cling. Another change that took place was the introduction of drawers for women. These had been a purely masculine garment, though there were reports that Catherine de' Medici (1519–89) had worn them. Most women considered them quite immodest, associating them with courtesans, actresses and dancers. However, with the new light dresses they became a necessity. The new fashions also brought a change in the centre of attraction, which shifted to the bosom. Bust improvers and false bosoms were often worn.

Many women enjoyed a new freedom with the loose-fitting dresses but this again was interpreted as loose morals.

Ladies' drawers, 1820. The legs are attached to a wide waistband and reach to just below the knee. There is no gusset.

CARICATURISTS POKED FUN at the fashions and their apparent transparency which revealed the lack of undergarments.

(Right) Pantalettes were longer than drawers and were trimmed with lace and tucks. The display of these lower parts was considered scandalous.

Bust improvers made of wadding and whalebone thrust the bosom upwards until, in some cases, the chin was in danger of being lost between the invading mounds!

(Above) Drawers were first worn by girls at the end of the 18th century, so, unusually, children set a fashion for the future.

busk

Masculine-looking undergarments, 1798, signalled the very beginnings of emancipation.

(Above) Wearing a false bosom with a low-cut dress needed care. They were made of wax or cotton and tied on with ribbons.

Discarding the corset was not a universal trend. This long-line corset laced at the back thrust the bosom upwards.

19

NECKCLOTHS AND CORSETS – 1790–1820

The Revolution affects men's clothes too, but it is sometimes painful . . .

Beau Brummell was the epitome of the perfect English gentleman.

Neckcloths and how they were tied were crucial. They were often so stiff they cut the skin.

BEING A DANDY in the early 19th century was a costly and often painful business. During the first two decades the ideal look was one of immaculate simplicity. Neckcloths had to be heavily starched and perfectly tied. Underwear had to be clean and fresh-smelling and outerwear superbly tailored. Unusually, personal cleanliness was now the mark of a perfect gentleman and many men took to wearing eau-de-cologne.

By 1820 the desired silhouette was somewhat effeminate and tiny waists were fashionable. Young men squeezed themselves into tight corsets and created a full bosom by inserting a small cushion under their clothes. A quizzing glass was *the* accessory and some die-hards even had their optic nerve loosened so that the glass became essential.

Dandies in late 18th-century France were called "Incroyables". Their dishevelled appearance symbolized the disorder of the French Revolution.

Ironing ensured that the corseted dandy had a starched collar as "stiff and smooth as a billiard board".

This pair of long drawers has two internal strings for tightening.

Drawers were short when worn under breeches and long when worn under pantaloons or trousers.

Under the underwear: toilet preparations now lasted for hours, where previously fashionable types had smelled of dirt or horseflesh.

Men, too, had to squeeze into corsets to be fashonable.

starched cravat

corset

(Above) The British Prince Regent who frightened his doctors by trying too hard to squash his portly figure into his corset.

calf pads

baggy trousers

(Right) A tiny waist, muffled neck and exaggerated bosom – the perfect dandy.

This young dandy of 1827 has white, baggy trousers, a nipped-in waist, long hair and a jauntily angled top hat. This somewhat effeminate look was called a "Poodle".

THERE WERE REPORTS that some young men wore their cravats so stiff that their ear lobes had been chopped off! Notice the quizzing glass.

Shoulder puffs or "support balloons" were attached with tapes to the shoulders of the chemise.

B Y 1820 WOMEN'S DRESS had once again assumed a more modest air with higher necklines and fuller skirts, and a new silhouette developed. Skirts became wider, sleeves fuller and the waist was whittled away so that by 1830 a fashionable woman looked like a wasp. The tight corsets and layers of petticoats required to achieve this look were very restricting, so when the crinoline was invented in 1856 it was greeted with enthusiasm. It was basically a hooped petticoat which supported the ever-widening skirts and so allowed women to abandon some of their suffocating layers of petticoats. It was a fashion worn and loved by women of all classes. Working girls wore crinolines to the factories and it was reported that girls in Prussia even wore them to work in the fields!

The crinoline did have its disadvantages, however. The slightest breeze caused the skirt to fly up and expose a pretty ankle to be seen by an observant gentleman. A high wind, on the other hand, might expose a modest lady still further, and many a young woman spent hours embroidering her underclothing for just such an occurrence, which led to a questioning of the morality of the garment in some quarters! This was a period of industrial expansion and the crinoline echoed this trend, becoming ever more exaggerated. By the end of the 1850s there was not room for two women to sit on the same sofa and there were numerous accidents.

The new "wasp" shape for women – enormous sleeves, tiny waists and ever-expanding skirts.

The dangers of tight lacing were very real and some fatalities were recorded. Waists were often reduced by up to 10 centimetres with stays.

The wasp required shoulder puffs to pad the sleeves, tightly laced corsets, and many stiff petticoats which immodestly showed the ankle.

A COTTON PETTICOAT with hoops sewn into it (below). Queen Victoria found the crinoline "indelicate, expensive, dangerous and hideous".

Crinolines came in many different guises. (Left) This horsehair-stiffened petticoat has flexible steel hoops inserted into it.

(Below) GRADUALLY the crinoline became flatter at the front with the fullness of the skirt at the back, making it more comfortable to wear.

THE INFLATABLE CRINOLINE, made of india-rubber tubes, could be blown up to the size required with a small air pump. The unfortunate had punctures!

BY 1860 the crinoline had expanded so much it was quite impractical.

This "cage" crinoline (left) is so-called because of its flexible steel hoops. It did away with the need for layers of heavy petticoats, so giving the wearer more freedom to walk. Red corsets became fashionable.

The crinoline was worn by all classes. Housemaids caused havoc, for instance breaking costly ornaments with a careless twirl.

23

STICKING OUT BEHIND – BUSTLES

The practice of padding the bottom has been with us for centuries.

FALSE "RUMPS" or "bums" appeared during the last quarter of the 18th century. Unlike 17th-century bum rolls, they were usually large pads stiffened with cork. A fashionable lady might go to a "bum shop" to be expertly fitted with the appropriate padding to give her silhouette the required shape.

(Left) In the early 1800s women often placed a small padded roll in the back of their gowns. Sometimes this resulted in a strange posture known as the Grecian bend.

(Right) Even the poorer classes used the "sausage" pad in order to be fashionable.

PADDING VARIOUS PARTS OF THE ANATOMY to achieve a desired shape has been the custom throughout history. One fashion accessory which has repeatedly reappeared is the bustle, a device worn to lift the skirt high at the rear and thus increase the size of the bottom. As early as 1343 an English monk complaind that women had loose morals because they had sewn fox-tails into their garments to pad out their bottoms. The bustle has appeared since in various guises. Sometimes it was a small pad or layers of stiff material tied around the waist, or it could form part of a petticoat, or even be a separate, cage-like structure.

When fashionable, the bustle was worn by all classes. Determined servant girls unable to afford the real thing resorted to stuffing dusters or newspapers up their skirts! There were practical problems for the fashionable lady, however. First, the bustle was liable to slip out of place, being situated in a region where it was difficult to keep an eye on it. Second, sitting down gracefully was an extremely tricky manoeuvre!

BUSTLES GRADUALLY became larger during the first part of the 19th century and varied in shape. One critical contemporary remarked that some women seemed to have some domestic utensil fastened under their dresses.

In the 1830s a flounced bustle was often worn over the petticoat which, coupled with an extremely tight corset, accentuated the waist.

horsehair
bustle

cage

(Left) The sewing machine was in more general use by the 1870s and this enabled a rich woman to display her wealth with yards of frills and flounces worn over the support of a bustle petticoat. This horsehair bustle of the 1870s shows how the fashion was achieved.

hoop

pivot

petticoat

metal bands

AN INGENIOUS contraption made of metal bands which worked on a pivot. It could be raised when sitting and automatically sprang back when the wearer stood up.

(Left) The bustle went out of fashion during the late 1870s and reappeared in the 1880s in a more angular form, giving a shelf-like appearance at the back. Some observers said it looked like a tea-tray.

(Above) This cotton bustle of the 1880s had an additional "cage" whose size could be altered with the lacings. The bustle petticoat was then tied on over underpetticoats with ribbon laces.

Reaction Against Restriction – 1850–1900

In a move to promote health, new styles of underwear appear.

In 1851 Mrs Amelia Bloomer advocated bloomers to free women from the discomforts of fashion.

THE REFORM MOVEMENT of the late 19th and early 20th centuries was a reaction against the harmful effects of fashion on health. Several influential people were involved. A group of artists called the Pre-Raphaelite Brotherhood worked to bring art back to nature and their ideas spilled over into dress. Only what was natural could be beautiful and this meant abandoning harmful corsets and adopting an "antique" (thick!) waist in its natural position.

Also important in the movement was Dr Gustav Jaeger's "wool next to the skin" theory. He claimed that only animal fibres stopped the retention of the "noxious exhalations" of the body and introduced his sanitary woollen underwear in the 1880s. He also felt that men were prone to draughts creeping up their trouser legs and that it would be healthier if they wore close-fitting breeches and stockings. The Reform Movement did not have universal appeal. Its fatal flaw was not recognizing that people do not dress just for health and warmth, but also to attract; and attractiveness is somehow lost in knitted drawers, woollen combinations and thick waists!

The medical profession was becoming increasingly concerned about the dangers of tight lacing. Curvature of the spine caused by restricting corsets was diagnosed frequently in the 1870s.

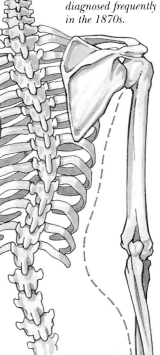

These shoulder braces for a girl of 8-10 were designed to ensure a good posture. Even children were not exempt from the cruelty of fashion.

VENUS (right), with her antique waist, was the role model for the Reformers. They advocated underwear like the corset bodice above, which was designed to support but not constrict the body.

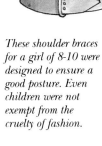

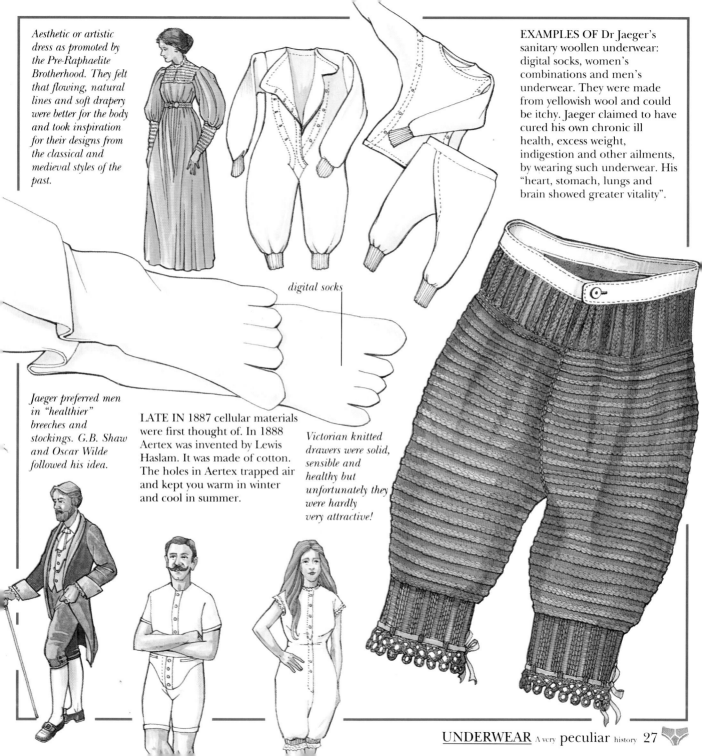

Aesthetic or artistic dress as promoted by the Pre-Raphaelite Brotherhood. They felt that flowing, natural lines and soft drapery were better for the body and took inspiration for their designs from the classical and medieval styles of the past.

EXAMPLES OF Dr Jaeger's sanitary woollen underwear: digital socks, women's combinations and men's underwear. They were made from yellowish wool and could be itchy. Jaeger claimed to have cured his own chronic ill health, excess weight, indigestion and other ailments, by wearing such underwear. His "heart, stomach, lungs and brain showed greater vitality".

digital socks

Jaeger preferred men in "healthier" breeches and stockings. G.B. Shaw and Oscar Wilde followed his idea.

LATE IN 1887 cellular materials were first thought of. In 1888 Aertex was invented by Lewis Haslam. It was made of cotton. The holes in Aertex trapped air and kept you warm in winter and cool in summer.

Victorian knitted drawers were solid, sensible and healthy but unfortunately they were hardly very attractive!

S-Bends, Suspenders and Seduction – 1900-1908

Women's underwear is frilly and extravagant while men's remains purely functional.

Ladies' combinations are fashionably frilly and elaborately trimmed with lace.

LUXURY AND EXTRAVAGANCE characterized women's underwear in the first decade of the 20th century. It was much lighter in appearance and feel and elaborately trimmed with flounces, frills and lace. The fashionable shape was the S-bend, made famous by the drawings of the American artist Charles Dana Gibson and the English actress Camille Clifford. A full bosom, a minute waist and large hips were required and to achieve this women had to endure another cruel corset. To have two bosoms was considered positively indecent, so seamstresses sewed tiny pillows inside the dress to pad out the cleavage.

Suspenders had first appeared in 1876 when French dancers, performing in London, had caused great excitement showing glimpses of naked thighs with suspenders stretched across them to hold up their stockings. Now they were in more general use, along with silk stockings which were often embroidered with fetching designs to catch the eye of any watchful gentleman hoping for sight of a pretty ankle. Men's underwear remained stoutly functional, but what it lacked in style it made up for in colour and stripes.

Underwear even found its way onto postcards.

THE S-BEND in profile. The long metal stays crushed the stomach and cut into the groin.

The ultimate in seduction. A tight corset, large bosom and black, silk stockings. The chemise is arranged awkwardly because of the suspenders.

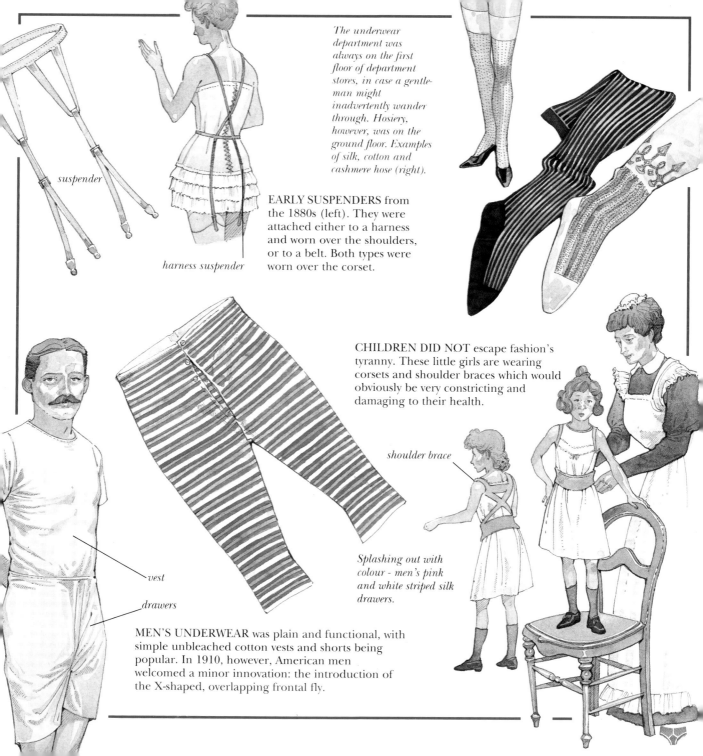

The underwear department was always on the first floor of department stores, in case a gentleman might inadvertently wander through. Hosiery, however, was on the ground floor. Examples of silk, cotton and cashmere hose (right).

suspender

harness suspender

EARLY SUSPENDERS from the 1880s (left). They were attached either to a harness and worn over the shoulders, or to a belt. Both types were worn over the corset.

CHILDREN DID NOT escape fashion's tyranny. These little girls are wearing corsets and shoulder braces which would obviously be very constricting and damaging to their health.

shoulder brace

Splashing out with colour - men's pink and white striped silk drawers.

vest

drawers

MEN'S UNDERWEAR was plain and functional, with simple unbleached cotton vests and shorts being popular. In 1910, however, American men welcomed a minor innovation: the introduction of the X-shaped, overlapping frontal fly.

SOME CAN, SOME SHOULDN'T – 1908–1918

Women go straighter and the brassière makes an appearance.

Dress designs by Paul Poiret (left). Their simple lines were radically different from previous luxurious fashions and the dresses were denounced as "mere" dishcloths by other designers.

"Some can, some shouldn't". A poster (left) from 1910 suggested that not everyone had the posterior for Poiret's designs.
(Right) A "Princess Petticoat" made of cambric with broderie anglaise and lace.

A SLIMMER LINE replaced the S-bend shape and the frothy, frilly petticoats, which began to disappear around 1907. This was partly due to the growing movement for women's emancipation. Another important factor was the influence of the young Parisian couturier Paul Poiret. He banished curves and claimed that he was liberating women from their corsets. It could hardly be called liberation, however, because at the same time he shackled their legs with his "hobble" skirt which was so restricting that women could only walk with short, mincing steps.

Bust improvers and boned bodices were still worn to supplement the deficiencies of nature and it was at this time that the brassière appeared. The first brassières did not look very different from bodices, but an innovation in design came from America. Caresse Crosby, an American debutante, designed a bra using two handkerchiefs and baby ribbon in 1914. It gave a natural separation to the bosoms and the design, patented in 1914, was later bought by the corset-makers Warner Brothers.

The new shape demanded a very long and nearly tubular corset, making it hard to sit down.

AN EXAMPLE of a hobble-skirted evening dress of 1917 which required a hobble-petticoat underneath. This had two steel hoops around the hip line. It would have been quite restricting for a successful tango!

Caresse Crosby's brassière was designed with the help of her French maid. It was revolutionary in that it separated the bosoms and left the midriff free. It was actually another revolt against restriction and soon all her friends wanted one!

boned bodice

Early brassières were very simple in style and did not separate but merely flattened the bosoms. Two examples above are a cotton Aertex brassière (left) and a boned bust bodice (right). Both date from about 1913.

Men remained unexciting and conservative in their vests, drawers and combinations and many still wore corsets, though these were usually called support belts. There was now a clear distinction between drawers and pants. "Pants" were either ankle-length or to mid-calf; "drawers" were just above or below the knee. The examples on the right are Jaeger garments and would have been made of wool.

combinations

vest

suspender belt

pants

Many young girls were still tightly restricted in corsets, but some experienced liberation when the corset was replaced by a suspender belt in 1916.

EMANCIPATION AND ELASTIC – 1918–1939

Slimline fashions demand rigorous figure control but underwear becomes more comfortable.

The flattened flapper with her boyish, straight-hipped figure was the ideal shape in the 1920s.

WOMEN'S EMANCIPATION after World War I had a profound effect on fashion. As women were now "equal" to men, there was a suppression of physical differences. Busts were flattened, hips were slimmed, waists were by-passed, hair was cropped and the ideal figure was a straight line. This boyish look gave way to a more elegant line in the 1930s but throughout the period the emphasis was on slimness. Technological advances meant that underwear was often more comfortable, with the increased use of elastic and the introduction of the zip fastener. The shorter skirts of the 1920s created a demand for flesh-coloured stockings to enhance newly exposed legs and in 1938 the first nylon stockings made an appearance at a New York World Fair. Changes were taking place in menswear too.

A number of combination garments appeared in the 1920s. The corselette (below), was a bra and corset in one.

Camiknickers were formed by uniting the camisole and knickers. At first they were called step-ins and were usually lace-trimmed.

These camiknickers have an integral belt made from a new material, lastex, which made dressing and undressing easier.

Brief bathing trunks for men were first glimpsed on the French Riviera in 1932 and from this came a new design in underpants. It offered a "No-gap opening with gentle support, elastic fibre, no buttons, no bulk, no binding". In 1934 Clark Gable was seen without a vest in the movie *It Happened One Night* and the modern fashion of wearing only briefs was born.

Flattener bras, essential for the shapeless look, were very restricting. But there were no protests on health grounds.

1930s' skirts were longer, but the desirable shape was still very slim. This look demanded controlling corsets.

The sizing of undergarments was introduced at this time. Different figure types were identified and everyone could be accommodated, even the mature figure. (Below) A corset is worn over combinations made from knitted rayon.

"Menswear" stated in 1935 that: "Underwear should have the grace of Apollo and the romance of Byron." (Left) A man's singlet vest and drawers from the 1930s!

stockings

suspenders

silk sheen

Stockings were usually made of silk and were now affordable by thousands of women who had earned money from war work. The silk's sheen drew attention to the legs.

combinations

American styles began to influence men's underwear and it became more colourful. (Left) Shorts in an "air-cooled" fabric similar to Aertex, which let the body breathe. (Right) Bright striped shorts with a seamless crotch and a cotton vest.

PARACHUTES AND PASSION KILLERS – THE 1940s

Wartime austerity means unglamorous underwear; then femininity returns.

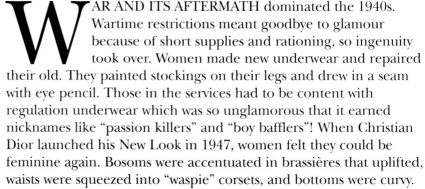

Glamour was what you made it and the advantage of painted-on stockings was that they did not ladder!

WAR AND ITS AFTERMATH dominated the 1940s. Wartime restrictions meant goodbye to glamour because of short supplies and rationing, so ingenuity took over. Women made new underwear and repaired their old. They painted stockings on their legs and drew in a seam with eye pencil. Those in the services had to be content with regulation underwear which was so unglamorous that it earned nicknames like "passion killers" and "boy bafflers"! When Christian Dior launched his New Look in 1947, women felt they could be feminine again. Bosoms were accentuated in brassières that uplifted, waists were squeezed into "waspie" corsets, and bottoms were curvy.

Although nylon had been patented and was in production before the war, its use did not become widespread until afterwards. In America nylon stockings were being produced on a national scale in 1940 and, later, were useful currency for American troops dating fashion-starved European girls. Men's underwear changed little, although in 1946 Jockey International patented the Y-front construction for men's pants.

KNITTING WAS a favourite black-out occupation and many women knitted under-garments for themselves.

THE FAMOUS "passion killers" issued to women in the armed forces came in khaki, navy, blue and grey.

INGENIOUS WOMEN often made underwear like these knickers from old curtain material or worn-out dresses.

knitted drawers

rayon passion killers

curtain material

Damaged parachutes were occasionally released from military to civilian hands. Women seized them for making underwear like this petticoat.

Men's vests (left) usually had a centre front opening. Underpants could be short or long. Combinations were still worn by some.

What women couldn't obtain, they could always dream about. (Right) An advertisement for black silk camiknickers.

Dior's ultra-feminine New Look (below) was eagerly adopted by women who were tired of the drab war years.

silk camiknickers

TO ACHIEVE the shape for the New Look, women wore the waspie (below), a short, boned corset, sometimes only 12-15 centimetres deep.

boned corset

wasp waist

The bra was now universally worn and came in different shapes. Stitching was added underneath or on top for those who needed uplift.

Jane Russell in the film "Outlaw". Her uplift bra set a fashion trend.

full skirt

There was a sensation on Wimbledon's centre court in 1949 when "Gorgeous Gussie" (Gussie Morgan) wore these eye-catching knickers.

STIFF BRAS AND PETTICOATS – THE 1950s

Glamour returns and again women squeeze themselves in and pad themselves out.

The most popular bra of the decade was known as the "sweater girl bra" (right).

padded girdle

The ideal was a high, pointed bosom quite unlike that which Nature intended. Padding, falsies and even inflatable bras like this were used to achieve the look.

calf pad worn under stockings

FASHION CAME TO LIFE again in the 1950s. The new, full, swirling skirts seemed symbolic of the new mood of optimism. Advertising laws were relaxed in the mid-1950s and it became possible to advertise underwear on television, which had a powerful influence in promoting new styles. Films also played their part, with actresses like Brigitte Bardot and Elizabeth Taylor seen in their undergarments. The widespread use of nylon completely revolutionized underwear, making beautiful garments affordable by all. There was also an improvement in elasticized materials, enabling manufacturers to produce garments with two-way stretch. Bosoms were "in" and so were falsies. With these went stiff petticoats and boned corsets, giving a structured and, once again, artificial look to female underwear.

Padded girdles to make bottoms curvy were bought by mail order. They had names like "Hips, hips hooray" and "Hippie helper".

For those with skinny calves, leg pads in moulded plastic were the answer and were worn under stockings. Haven't we seen these somewhere before?

Very full skirts were held out either with wiring or by stiffened layers of petticoats. In 1950 paper nylon petticoats were often worn for dancing.

sheath dress

restricting corset

Later in the decade the sheath dress became fashionable. It showed every curve of the figure and demanded constricting undergarments (right).

Men's underwear changed very little. (Right) "Superman" models a singlet and Y-fronts, which were advertised as the "finest support underwear".

singlet

Y FRONT

Y-fronts

(Right) Longline bras, laced corsets and corsets with an "uplifting" underbelt were used to control heavier figures.

Hollywood influenced fashion and underwear. For example, baby doll pyjamas (left) became fashionable after the film "Baby Doll" in 1956.

baby doll pyjamas

The dread of all teenage girls was fleecy-lined school knickers. Unfeminine and hot to wear, they came in ghastly "school" colours such as maroon, bottle green, grey and brown.

school knickers

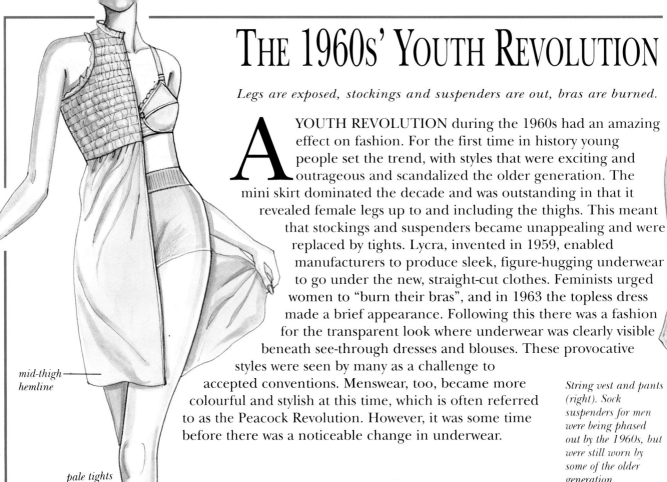

THE 1960s' YOUTH REVOLUTION

Legs are exposed, stockings and suspenders are out, bras are burned.

A YOUTH REVOLUTION during the 1960s had an amazing effect on fashion. For the first time in history young people set the trend, with styles that were exciting and outrageous and scandalized the older generation. The mini skirt dominated the decade and was outstanding in that it revealed female legs up to and including the thighs. This meant that stockings and suspenders became unappealing and were replaced by tights. Lycra, invented in 1959, enabled manufacturers to produce sleek, figure-hugging underwear to go under the new, straight-cut clothes. Feminists urged women to "burn their bras", and in 1963 the topless dress made a brief appearance. Following this there was a fashion for the transparent look where underwear was clearly visible beneath see-through dresses and blouses. These provocative styles were seen by many as a challenge to accepted conventions. Menswear, too, became more colourful and stylish at this time, which is often referred to as the Peacock Revolution. However, it was some time before there was a noticeable change in underwear.

mid-thigh hemline

String vest and pants (right). Sock suspenders for men were being phased out by the 1960s, but were still worn by some of the older generation.

pale tights

IT WAS FASHIONABLE to be young and very thin. Underwear companies began to manufacture a range of garments specifically for teenagers, recognizing a new assertive generation of girls with definite ideas about what they wanted to wear.

MORE WIDESPREAD use of Lycra meant co-ordinated underwear sets. Available in the early 1960s, these did not become prominent until late in the decade.

"little girl" bar shoes

The topless dress was matched by a topless bathing suit (second from left).

Bolder colours were used for underwear, demonstrating the influence of Pop Art on fashion.

The plunging, padded "Wonderbra", introduced in 1969, drew new attention to the bosom.

Tights, essential with the mini dress, were often brightly coloured.

CONTRADICTION AND CONFUSION – THE 1970s

Underwear styles reflect a struggle between feminism and femininity.

CONFUSION REIGNED IN THE FASHION WORLD in the 1970s. Hemlines went up and down, with mini and maxi skirts, hot pants and flared trousers appearing together. Bra and corset sales slumped, and yet there was a revival of interest in glamorous underwear. An American research project aimed to find out "What Happened to the Girdle?" and found that some women refused to wear one because men "liked a behind with a wiggle"! At the same time many women admitted that they preferred having their bottoms shaped by an undergarment. Jeans became a universal fashion and were often skin-tight, and so natural bottoms were the focus of attention for the first time in history. Figure-hugging jersey dresses were also popular, demanding ultra-smooth, natural-looking underwear. Tights with built-in panties and bodyshapers helped to provide a sleeker look, but the biggest advances came with the introduction of moulded underwear in the mid-1970s. Garments were manufactured from a single piece of material and moulded into shape, giving the natural "no underwear" appearance required.

Colour and style reached men's underwear at last.

FIGURE-HUGGING dresses revealed the female shape in a similar way to the medieval dress on page 11. Women demanded underwear that would control but be invisible.

AN EXAMPLE OF moulded underwear that gave an ultra-smooth line. The ultimate in invisible foundation wear, it was very different from the glamorous "Wonderbra" that was also popular.

Janet Reger became world-famous in the 1970s for her lacy, feminine underwear sets. They were designed to be attractive and sensuous and quite the opposite to the practical appearance of moulded underwear.

Colourful, stretch-nylon hipsters for men. They were advertised as being "more brief, clingy and fashion conscious than ever before".

Many men preferred T-shirts to vests, available in different colours, with underpants to match.

A stick-on bra, "with no straps, hidden wires or bones", guaranteed to "hold and mould you".

STOCKINGS AND suspenders made a come-back in the late 1970s. They were worn by many young women who saw them as glamorous. Lacy bra and brief sets like this one from 1976 were also popular.

FITNESS AND POWER – THE 1980S TO THE PRESENT

Sport influences underwear design and glamorous corsets make a come-back.

The new, active life created a demand for sports bras.

Modern man turns to the gym to alter his body shape, and then adorns it with figure-hugging underwear that is more glamorous than practical.

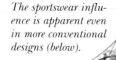

Cropped tops and simple cotton briefs were popular, demonstrating the influence of sportswear.

The sportswear influence is apparent even in more conventional designs (below).

(Above) A design straight from the boxing ring: boxer shorts in bright colours.

Combinations for men have returned, but are now called bodysuits. Made in stretch cotton, they are simple in style and are designed to emphasize the new, fit, muscular body.

THE HEALTH AND FITNESS boom of the 1980s and early 1990s had a considerable effect on underclothing. A suntanned and muscular body was seen as symbolic of success and power, and there was a demand for clothes that fitted like a second skin. Lycra provided these, and underwear designs reflected the influence of sportswear. Another important phenomenon was the rise of the female executive, with many women reaching top positions, one particular example being the British Prime Minister, Margaret Thatcher. Female fashions mirrored this by becoming more aggressive-looking, with straight lines and padded shoulders and softly padded underwear beneath.

In contrast to the smooth lines of Lycra-based underwear, there has been a revival of interest in glamorous lacy and boned corsets and long-line bras. These are more decorative than torturous, however, with the 1990s' woman preferring to display rather than constrict her body. On the catwalk, fashion designers have frequently shown underwear as outerwear with both men and women encased in corsets. If we look at the Cretan goddess in her corset on page 8, we could wonder whether this is a return to where we started . . . and so our story must end.

Shoulder pads (below) often extended to underwear. This look, called "power dressing" echoed the rise of the female executive.

cone-shaped bust

(Left) The pop star Madonna wearing a Jean Paul Gaultier-designed corset as outerwear. The corset seaming emphasizes her fit and muscular body, but at the same time she appears to be in defensive armour-plating. Madonna started a new fashion for the "bustier" top.

seams

GLAMOROUS UNDERWEAR with the accent on luxury rather than practicality (left) appealed to young women who had never worn a corset and therefore saw it as frivolous rather than restricting. Advances in technology have meant that an Edwardian-style look can be enjoyed without the torture!

(Right) A 1990s Gaultier design that owes much to the past and demands a perfect physique. Men's tights and padded codpiece from the 16th century and a cravat reminiscent of those worn by 19th-century dandies. But will men wear outfits like this in broad daylight?

cravat

Underwear is often seen as outerwear on the catwalk. Men and women parade in corsets and girdles that are designed to define rather than constrict the body. Corsetry lacing has also returned as decoration on vests, bras and cropped tops.

corset

codpiece

Underwear FACTS

Underwear can cause agony and embarrassment.

Causing a miscarriage . . .
The rigid look of 16th-century women's fashions was achieved by placing a busk – a long pointed piece of bone, metal or whalebone – in the centre front of the corset. These busks were an intimate part of a woman's dress and were often given to her as love tokens. It was suggested that they were so constricting that they produced miscarriages and were worn by women of easy virtue precisely for that purpose.

Stuck in a doorway . . .
In 1616 James I of England tried to forbid cartwheel farthingales as they took up too much space. In the same year there was an accident when a number of guests going to a masque became wedged in the entrance hall.

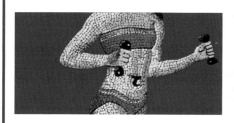

Riding with no drawers . . .
In the 17th century a skirt worn with no drawers was considered sufficient apparel for horseriding. This gave rise to a number of mishaps. Louis XIV was said to be thoroughly amused when, on two separate occasions, ladies tumbled from their horses and landed in compromising positions.

Oh, for the real thing . . . !
In 1786 so many artificial accessories were worn that one English lady, when undressing, had to ask her maid to " . . . put my bosom on the chair and the hips above it. Take care of my bottom and don't ruffle it. Lay this eye on to my dressing box and lock up my teeth in the cloth bag . . . "

The truth will out . . .
A French captain, in his memoirs, described how he entered Paris in 1809 with Napoleon's army and was overjoyed to be promoted to a higher rank. Unfortunately, his new rank meant that he was obliged to wear white silk stockings and the poor man, not having muscular calves, had to

resort to padding. He had to attend an important banquet and, for the occasion, wore a pair of under-hose, calf pads, a second pair of stockings to smooth out the edges and finally the white silk over-stockings. He made a great impression on a young lady at the feast, but her interest in him quickly evaporated in the bedroom after he had smuggled his calf pads under the pillow and it was revealed that he was really a spindle-shanks!

Men strangle themselves . . .
For the 19th-century dandies an alternative form of neckwear to the cravat was the stock. This was a band of horsehair or buckram which was sometimes edged with leather and fastened at the back with a buckle, hook and eye. The idea was to give the wearer a look of "hauteur and greatness" but in doing so they held the head rigid,

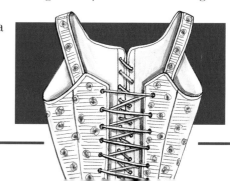

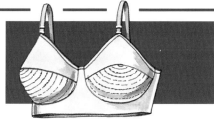

constricted the throat and caused weals on the skin.

Dying for fashion . . .
In 1814 it was reported that the British Prince Regent was very upset as his doctors had ordered him to give up wearing his stays as they were so tight they would kill him.

Premature wrinkles . . .
In 1826 in Paris, very young ladies were seen with "frightful wrinkles" on their upper chests. These were caused by the continual wearing of corsets that pushed their bosoms up too high.

An explosion . . .
In 1828 an English tradesman recorded that his daughter's stays were so tight that when she tried to bend down they gave way with a tremendous explosion and she fell to the ground convincing him that she had snapped in two.

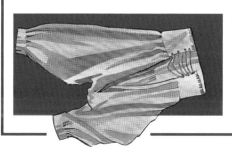

Crinolines save lives . . .
In America the *Hampshire Gazette* reported in May 1862 that several ladies had been kept afloat in the sea by their crinoline frames until help arrived after a boating accident. In the same year a woman attempted to commit suicide from the Clifton Suspension Bridge in Bristol, but she parachuted to safety in her crinoline!

Crinolines cause havoc . . .
In 1863 2,000 women were burnt to death in the Cathedral of Santiago, Spain, when candles ignited their flimsy dresses worn over crinolines. In the same year an English pottery lost £200 worth of articles which were swept down by the crinolines of their workwomen.

Teenage agony . . .
A lady writing in 1867 recalled that, at her fashionable London school, it was the custom for the waists of the pupils to be reduced two centimetres a month until they were considered small enough by the lady principal. Every morning her dressing was

supervised by a maid, to ensure that her corset was tight enough. At 17, her waist measured only 32 centimetres!

Fatal fashion . . .
In 1874 Luke Linmer wrote a widely-read treatise on the dangers of fashion. He listed 97 "diseases" ascribed to the wearing of stays and corsets. These included: sleepiness, apoplexy, whooping cough, consumption, ugly children, dropsy of the belly and epilepsy.

Oh, for a tiny waist . . . !
It is claimed that in 1895 very vain ladies had their two lowest ribs removed in order to obtain a small waist. Others relied on the tight corset which damaged the liver by pushing it upwards into the lungs and making breathing practically impossible. This achieved the much sought after heaving bosom.

GLOSSARY

Bloomers Long, baggy, Turkish-style trousers worn by dress reformer Amelia Bloomer in the 19th century.

Bombast Padding of horsehair, cotton-wool or bran used to stuff breeches in the 16th and 17th centuries.

Braies A loose, trouser-like garment worn by men in medieval times.

Brassière A garment worn to bind, or later to support and uplift, the breasts.

Bum roll A roll of padding worn under the skirt at the waist, to make the dress stand out at the back.

Bust improver Padding sewn into or inserted into pockets in a dress to augment the bust.

Busk A piece of wood, whalebone, ivory or horn that was slotted into the front of a corset to stiffen it.

Bustle An artificial structure giving extension and fullness to the skirt at the back.

Calf pad Padding worn under stockings to simulate muscular calves.

Camiknickers Camisole or chemise and French knickers combined. At first these were called "step-ins".

Camisole Derived from the French word for bed-jacket or loose corset tied at the front with ribbons.

Chemise Female smock or shift, worn next to the skin.

Codpiece A pouch worn to cover the genitals. The word cod originally meant a bag or an envelope and codpieces were frequently used as purses or places to keep sweetmeats. The Church banned them in the 16th century.

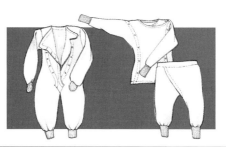

Corset Worn by both sexes to narrow the waist and correct the posture.

Crinoline A petticoat with hoops of cane, whalebone or steel (19th century).

Cropped top A stretch bra in the form of a short, tight-fitting vest.

Doublet A man's jacket worn in the 15th, 16th and 17th centuries.

Drawers Two tubes of material sewn on to a waistband and left open at the crotch.

Farthingale A hooped petticoat. The Spanish farthingale gave the dress a bell shape; the French farthingale made the dress stand out like a cartwheel from the waist.

Fascia Binding used to cover the breasts in ancient Greece.

Flattener bra A bra designed to flatten the breasts in the 1920s, when it was unfashionable to have any.

French knickers Short, full knickers, elasticated at the waist.

Garter Ribbon or band worn around the leg to keep the stockings up.

Hobble skirt A skirt that came tight into the ankles and forced a woman to walk with short, mincing steps.

Jockeys Short, close-fitting underpants worn by men.

Kalasiris A tight-fitting robe worn by Egyptian women.

Knickers An abbreviation for knickerbockers. A term used for drawers which were closed at the crotch.

Loincloth A brief garment worn around the loins by ancient peoples.

Moulded underwear Underwear manufactured from a single piece of material and moulded into shape giving a "no underwear" appearance.

Nylons A popular term for nylon stockings in the 1940s and 1950s.

Pannier A French term for 18th-century side hoops which were worn to give width to the hips.

Pantalettes Frilled, ankle-length covering worn by women in the early 19th century.

Passion killers Thick pants issued to women in the services.

Peasecod belly A term used to describe the padded belly of a man's doublet in the 16th century.

Points Laces, usually made from ribbon, used for tying one garment to another.

Quizzing glass A small monocle which was an important fashion accessory for the dandy in the early 19th century.

S-bend corset A corset designed to crush the stomach and cut into the groin, giving the wearer an S-shaped silhouette.

Sleeve support Also called support balloons – pads of linen or cotton stuffed with down and used to pad sleeves in the 1830s.

Stays 17th- and 18th-century term for a boned underbodice. The term also applied to the stiff inserts of whalebone or steel that were used to shape the garment.

Stock Stiff neckband worn by men in the 19th century as an alternative to the caravat.

Strophium A breast band worn by Roman ladies and used as a pocket.

Suspender An elastic strap with a fastener at the end, used to hold up women's stockings or men's socks. They were first worn by French dancers.

Waspie A term applied to the belt-like corsets of the late 1940s and 1950s, designed to create a tiny waist.

X-front The X-shaped overlapping frontal fly on men's underpants, introduced in America in 1910.

Y-front The Y-shaped fly patented by Jockey in 1946.

Zoné A girdle worn by women in ancient Greece.

INDEX

Artists

David Antram, pages 10-11, 12-13, 18-19, 26-27; Ray Burrows, page 24-25; Virginia Gray, pages 14-15, 16-17, 32-33, 34-35, 36-37, 38-39, 40-41, 42-43; John James, page 28-29; Joe McEwan, page 8-9; Lee Peters, page 22-23; Ron Tiner, page 20-21; Gerald Wood, page 30-31.